From the Heart

Other Works by the Author

The Into the Light Collection:

Into the Light: A Simple Way to Pray with the Sick and the Dying
Into the Light Study Guide
When I'm Alone: Thoughts and Prayers That Comfort
Near Life's End: What Family and Friends Can Do
A Time to Mourn: Recovering from the Death of a Loved One

The Times of Change, Times of Challenge series:

When You Are Getting Married
When Your Child Is Baptized
When You Are Facing Surgery
When an Aging Loved One Needs Care

The Breath of Life
The Hunger of the Heart
Alone with God

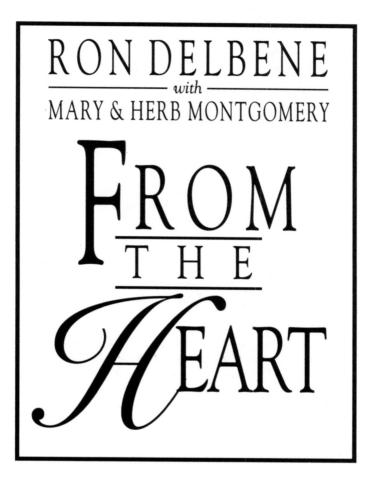

RON DELBENE
with
MARY & HERB MONTGOMERY

FROM THE HEART

UPPER ROOM BOOKS

NASHVILLE

FROM THE HEART

The epigraph is an excerpt from "Spiritual Formation—A Matter of the Heart," by Mary A. Avram, Director of Spiritual Formation, Scarritt-Bennett Center. Originally appeared in *Arches,* Fall 1990. Used by permission of the author.

Cover Design: Jim Bateman
Book Design: Richard Cook
First Printing: March 1991 (7)
Library of Congress Catalog Number: 90-71861
ISBN: 0-8358-0631-6

Printed in the United States of America

TO THE MANY PEOPLE WHO HAVE LISTENED TO

MY STORIES

AND SHARED THEIRS WITH ME.

THROUGH OUR SHARING WE HAVE BECOME

PART OF ONE ANOTHER'S LIVES.

AND ESPECIALLY TO MY FRIEND DALE,

WHOSE GIFT TO ME IS A CONSTANT REMINDER

OF WHO I AM CALLED TO BE.

It is the heart that loves and wills, that weeps and breaks. It is the door of the heart on which Jesus knocks in Revelation 3:20 and it is from the overflow of the heart that the mouth speaks in St. Luke 6. It is the heart that is restless and hungers to 'know' God and be formed and filled with the fullness of God.

Mary A. Avram

Contents

Appendix

Introduction

During a presentation at a conference, I
realized I was sharing stories that some of my colleagues in
the audience had heard before. Later over lunch, I
apologized for the repetition, saying I hoped I hadn't bored
any of them.

With a laugh, one of my fellow pastors said, "Can't you
just imagine Jesus getting up to preach with Peter and John
in the audience? Jesus is only a couple of minutes into his
preaching when Peter leans toward John and grouses, 'Here
we go again with that one about the kid who wants his
inheritance so he can leave home.'"

This pastor's remark made me aware that although Jesus
preached for three years, scripture doesn't contain a large
number of his stories. Perhaps that's because instead of
telling a great many stories, Jesus often repeated those that
carried his message best. Naturally, those were the ones the
authors of the Gospels included in their writings.

Jesus' stories came out of the lives of the ordinary people
of his time: a woman baking bread and a shepherd
searching for a lost sheep; a rich young man looking for
direction and disgruntled laborers working in a vineyard.
The parables Jesus so frequently used required that his
listeners discover the meaning as it applied to their own
lives. Even today the parables remain open to interpretation
and personal application.

Actually, our entire faith history has been handed down
to us because our earliest forebears told stories that passed
from one generation to the next. After many years of being

shared in the oral tradition, the stories were recorded in the Hebrew Testament scrolls. Later, the same process took place in writing the Christian Testament.

God's story does not, however, end with what is included in the scriptures. At baptism we are dipped into God's storybook and thus become part of faith history. As we try to discern and live out the yearning of God, we become the living scriptures. We are part of a story that continues to grow and evolve. Every time we right an injustice, feed the hungry, or comfort the lonely, we act as a channel through which the love of God flows and the good news is proclaimed.

Telling people my story and listening to theirs is my way of walking with them, of being companions on the way. Through the sharing of stories, we put our joys and sorrows in perspective and open our eyes to the ways in which God is present in the ordinary circumstances of our lives and in the lives of those around us. This book is an invitation to walk with me and listen to my stories. Take from them what you will and let them trigger stories of your own which you, in turn, share with others. All of our stories together make up God's storybook, that fascinating, ongoing drama that is our faith history.

Author's Note: The stories in this book are true. With the exception of stories about my daughter, Anne, and my friends Taylor and Dale, personal names and some details have been changed to protect the privacy of the individuals involved.

Out of the Storeroom of Our Experiences

People come to ministers, pastoral counselors, and other caregivers with difficult and wide-ranging problems. Frequently we confront the fact that much of life is beyond our control. Even though I understood this in my head, it didn't really affect my whole being until I came face-to-face with the illness of my daughter.

Anne is a lively, inquisitive young woman who, for every answer you give her, has three more questions. She loves to go to camp, to sing, and to play guitar. A lover of sports, she particularly enjoys playing tennis and basketball and is an avid rock climber. At age fifteen, she developed a condition that rendered her left leg paralyzed and for the past two-and-a-half years has been in and out of a wheelchair. During this time I have learned what it means to be one of the wounded, one of the un-able.

I was brought up to think—and always believed—that I could fix things. Around home I am a handyman, able to repair everything from a torn screen to a dripping faucet. During my years of counseling and consulting I have become known for my ability to analyze situations and suggest solutions. But with Anne's condition, I came up against something I could not fix and for which I had no answers.

Caught up in a problem we didn't really understand, Eleanor, Anne, and I went from one specialist to another in the hope of finding a cause that might lead to a cure.

Appointments had to be scheduled at inconvenient times and medical decisions made when we felt unqualified to make them. Several times we were relieved to find out that Anne's problem was not a disease that was suspected. But that left us knowing only what it was not; no one could tell us what it was. We had a feeling of powerlessness and a sense that we were no longer in control of our lives.

Even though we tried to stay open to the present, the fear of an uncertain future loomed like a storm on the horizon. Weeks passed. Then months. Dealing with the wheelchair was frustrating and inconvenient for all of us. At home the bathroom could no longer have a door. Walls got scraped. If I wanted to hug Anne, I had to bend awkwardly to be at her level and invariably we bumped our eyeglasses. Whenever we went anywhere, the wheelchair had to be hauled up and down the fifteen stairs to our house. Once when we pulled into a handicap parking spot and discovered that the ramp was directly in front of the car, we wondered what fool had planned a parking lot that way. In a very short time, we became aware of just how much of life is inaccessible to the handicapped.

Nothing in our lives was as clear as it had once been. Unable to fix the situation, I became increasingly conscious of the uncertainty of life. Through all the anxiety and confusion, Eleanor, Anne, and I struggled to be aware of God's presence. We found strength by sharing our feelings with one another and praying together. Although we appreciated the interest and concern shown to us, people's questions sometimes pushed us more and more to try to explain the unexplainable.

The uncertainty about Anne's condition continues. Although she at times makes progress, she also has episodes that appear to be setbacks. For me, the experience has given new meaning to that line from Matthew's Gospel, "A householder brings out from his storeroom things both new and old" (Matt. 13:52, JB). Now when I share with people, there are new things that I bring from my storeroom of experience. I am better able to identify with the pain and disappointment of others. I know firsthand what it's like to be off balance while trying to embrace the moment and the present situation. My experience has taught me that life goes on and to miss any of it is a mistake. In times of anguish as well as in times of joy, I have known God's presence. What I have come to understand is that I am not called to fix life; I am simply called to live it.

I Know My Own and My Own Know Me

The first sermon I ever preached was on Good Shepherd Sunday. Not knowing anything about sheep and shepherds, I did a little research. At the end of the sermon, I said, "Every year our lectionary provides the opportunity to preach about Jesus as a shepherd, so I'm going to need a lifelong supply of ideas relating to that scripture. If any of you have stories about sheep or shepherds, I would love to hear them."

After the service, several people came up and shared their stories. The person I remember most vividly was an elderly gentleman who spoke with a British accent. He was well over six feet tall and thin as a drinking straw. Dressed as he was in a double-breasted, gray suit with a black pinstripe, he reminded me of Ichabod Crane. I mention these details because every time I tell a story someone has shared with me, I instantly visualize that person. There's a regular slide show going on in my head when I tell one shared story after another.

At any rate, this tall, slender gentleman told me that during the war he had been in British intelligence. During a critical point in the fighting, British operatives discovered that spies disguised as shepherds were getting through a particular mountain pass on the Turkish border. The British could not distinguish the impostors from the real shepherds who were tending their sheep in the area.

Knowing where the spies were coming through and not

being able to catch them was extremely frustrating. Then someone in British intelligence came up with the idea of using small planes to buzz the sheep. The plan was put into action and pilots flew in low over the mountain passes. The frightened sheep ran to their shepherds, clustering close around them. Anyone dressed as a shepherd with no sheep nearby was a spy.

How clever! How amazing! And how true to the Gospel of John in which Jesus says, "I am the good shepherd; I know my own and my own know me." (John 10:14-15, RSV).

A Need to Tell Their Story

❧

In my years as a pastor and a spiritual director, I have come to see that everyone has a story to tell. Sometimes the need to tell it is especially compelling. This was the case with Sarah, a recently widowed woman in a parish where I was the pastor.

Sarah's husband died while I was out of town speaking at a conference. I couldn't leave early because it was a small conference and there was no one to stand in for me. I called and explained my situation to Sarah, who agreed to postpone the funeral until I arrived. As soon as I got off the plane, I went to the funeral home where the service was ready to begin. All I knew about the circumstances of the death was that Sarah had awakened one morning and found Charlie dead beside her.

After the burial, Sarah left to spend some time with her son in another town, so I didn't have a chance to talk to her. But when she got back, I paid her a visit. She bustled around serving us tea before settling into an antique velvet chair with white crocheted arm protectors. The chair stood in a bay window that looked out on the budding spring woods of Sarah's country location. For a while we talked in generalities, then lapsed into silence. Sarah had lost interest in her tea and sat gazing out the window.

"Sarah," I said, "what was it like? Tell me about that morning."

She turned to face me, the light from the window making a silver halo of her gray hair. Tears shimmered in her eyes.

"Thank you for asking," she said. "I've been wishing someone would."

Sarah spoke slowly, as though trying to recapture every detail. She recalled what they had eaten for dinner that evening, the television shows they had watched, a joke Charlie had told her. Then she explained how upon awakening in the morning she had given her husband a little nudge and said, "Come on, Charlie. It's time to get up." When he didn't respond, she instinctively knew that he was dead. Even so, she got up and tried to wake him. "And then," she said in a voice just above a whisper, "I did a terrible thing."

With that, she grew very quiet. When it became clear she was not going to elaborate, I asked, "What could be that terrible, Sarah?"

She seemed to see the scene being played out in her mind's eye as she said, "I made myself a cup of tea. And for twenty minutes I just sat and drank tea because I couldn't think of what to do!"

"Then I remembered that I should call the paramedics. But I knew Charlie was already dead, so why would I do that? That's when I decided to call the ambulance." She closed her eyes and shuddered at the memory. "It was so horrible having to sit here in the living room and let the medical people work on him when I knew it was no use."

When Sarah finished her story, I told her that I was pleased she had shared it with me.

"My children won't let me talk about the circumstances of their father's death," she said. "No matter how hard I try, they keep saying, 'No, Mother, we don't want to hear anything about that. We just want to remember Daddy the way he was.'" Sarah sighed with relief. "Thank you, Ron, for asking me to tell my story."

Inviting people to tell their stories is a gift that is ours to give. After Sarah had told her story, her grief could begin to heal.

Where Is God?

Lester was a businessman in his sixties

who had lived in Sarasota all his life and had been a
founding member of the parish. His mother, who was in her
mid-eighties, lived in a nursing home near the church.
Every Wednesday Lester and his wife, Ellen, picked her up
and brought her to the church supper. And every Sunday
morning they brought her to the eleven o'clock service
even though she was not always clear about where she was
or who was who. I always made it a point to give her a big
hug and tell her how nice she looked. Lester said that she
used to say, "Oh, I just love getting hugs. Who is that
person?"

We agreed that real progress was being made when she
recognized me enough to say, "I just love that bearded
priest."

One Wednesday at the church supper Lester took me
aside, obviously wanting to tell me something in
confidence. "I think you should know that mother was
incontinent in church last Sunday," he said. "After the other
parishioners left, Ellen and I used a choir robe to get her to
the car. The robe is at the cleaners now. After I pick it up
tomorrow I'll return it to the church."

That, however, was only part of Lester's story. He
wanted me to know what was being done to prevent such
an occurrence in the future.

"Mother is going to start wearing absorbent underwear
to church," he said. "In case you and your staff wonder
where the extra boxes of these in the restrooms came

from, I bought them and Ellen and I put them there. Anyone with the same problem Mother has is welcome to use them."

Whenever I think of Lester, I am reminded that in order to find God, I don't have to look very far. God is in the love Lester has for his mother, in the patient understanding of his wife, in the gentle persistence of a woman suffering the ravages of aging. And when I think of those boxes in the restrooms, I see the graciousness of God in the sensitivity of a man who thought to make them available for anyone who might need them.

No Hotline to Heaven

❧

As I stood in the back of the church

one Sunday, silver-haired Emily asked if she could have a few words with me in private. A stylishly dressed woman in her sixties, she informed me matter-of-factly that she was going into the hospital the following day for a biopsy. Without disclosing the nature of her problem, she said, "I won't know about surgery until I get the report, but I wanted to tell you this morning so you could be praying that the test comes out negative. I know you have a direct line to God, and I want the best connection I can get."

Emily's request brought to mind how, as a newly ordained pastor, I felt good when somebody said I had a more direct line than they did. In those days I was eager to be perceived as a person of prayer who had the members of his congregation on his mind and in his heart. But as I became more experienced, my stomach tightened whenever someone implied that I had "a hotline to heaven." I wanted to protest that my line was no more direct than anyone else's. Now my perspective has shifted again. I've come to understand that Emily and others like her want to believe that pastors have a special connection because of their deep need to feel that someone is really serious about prayer and about developing a close relationship with God.

Although I appreciate that my access to God is no greater than anyone else's, I know that as a pastor I *should* be "on the line," and attentive to being there. After all, every vocation carries with it certain expectations and obligations: I expect my doctor to know more about medicine than I do, my attorney to be more knowledgeable about the law than I am, and my accountant to know more about taxes than I do. Parishioners, then, have a right to expect their pastor to be more knowledgeable about and attentive to prayer than they perhaps are. I don't believe anyone has expressed my views about prayer and the ministry better than Thomas Hooker, the famous preacher from America's colonial days who believed that prayer is the principal work of ministers and that it is by prayer that we must carry on the rest.

Here Comes Jesus!

Early in my ministry, I served a church where my responsibilities included the religious education of the children. Each Sunday morning I went from class to class and told about the scripture story of the day. I spent from five to ten minutes in each classroom and then left to let the teacher continue with the lesson.

This church was in the South, so typically the classrooms opened to the outside with large windows lining the walls. One Sunday as I walked past the windows of the preschool room, a little boy cried, "Get ready. Here comes Jesus!"

At the time, I found the remark amusing. Having a full beard and dressed as I was in my white robe, I probably did look like pictures of Jesus the child had seen. But as I thought about the incident, I felt uncomfortable being mistaken for Jesus. So the next time I met with my spiritual director, I told him what had happened and my feelings about it.

"How do you interact with those young children when you go into the classroom?" he asked.

"I give them each a hug. Usually two of them share my lap while I'm telling the story to the group."

"What you are saying puts me in mind of the scripture about Jesus calling the children," he said. "Remember, Ron, to those children you *are* Jesus. I wouldn't be surprised if some of these kids look back one day and wonder if they really did meet him."

Meet Jesus? Through me?

When I left that meeting I no longer felt uncomfortable

about being mistaken for Jesus by a preschooler. Instead I found myself asking, *What am I doing each day to be more like Jesus?* It's a humbling question and one that has served me well over the years when I take inventory of myself and my ministry.

With Them in Prayer

After Sunday worship services, we

hold a healing service in a side chapel of the church I am
currently serving. Parishioners who have pressing
problems or needs come to the communion rail. We stand
facing one another and they share what they would like me
to pray for. Then they kneel and I place my hands on top
of each person's head as I say a prayer for his or her
intention.

One Sunday Sam and Louise asked that I pray especially
for them that afternoon because they were going to visit
their daughter and son-in-law. Some troublesome issues
had to be discussed, and they were extremely anxious about
the meeting. After we prayed they got up from their knees
and expressed their appreciation.

"What time will the meeting take place?" I asked.

"We'll get there about three o'clock," Sam replied.
"They know something's up, so I suppose we'll start
talking soon after we arrive."

My watch has an alarm, and as we stood there I
explained that I was setting it for three-fifteen. "I know that
this will be a time of intense emotion, so when the alarm
goes off I'll be in prayer with you."

"That will be wonderful!" Louise said. She smiled
appreciatively, and the tension on Sam's face eased. They
knew they wouldn't be facing their situation alone; I would
be with them in prayer.

That afternoon Eleanor and the kids and I went to an
early movie. We were sitting in the darkened theater when

my alarm beeped. I quickly shut it off, closed my eyes, and pictured Sam and Louise. While holding them in my mind and heart, I asked God to guide and strengthen them as they carried out their difficult task.

The following week Louise called. "I just want to tell you," she said, "that when we got to our daughter's house I looked at my watch and it was three o'clock. I said to Sam, 'Ron is going to be remembering us in fifteen minutes, so let's go.'"

We've all had people promise to pray for us and then wondered if they really did. Or we've said we would pray for someone, then forgotten completely. Setting the alarm on my watch guards against this tendency. In the years since I began this habit, the alarm has gone off many times when I've been in a meeting. If it happens in staff meetings, everyone is used to it. When the person I'm praying for is known to the group, I'll say, "Let's remember Kate, who's in surgery right now," or "Let's pray together for John, who's having a job interview." Then for a few moments we sit in silent prayer and ask that God be present to that person in a special way. In other settings I simply shut the alarm off and briefly hold the person in my mind and heart.

Those of us who are pastors or who serve in other caregiving capacities are limited in the amount of time we can spend with our people; we can walk with them only part of the way. But prayer enables us to transcend our limitations of time and space and be present to anyone, anywhere, at any time. Through prayer we strengthen and sustain one another. Through prayer we are united with the people to whom we minister and with our God.

Through Our Woundedness

My friendship with Taylor spanned a
decade, and during a portion of those years we tried to meet
twice a month. We couldn't always make it, but when we
did our times together were filled with talk—talk of our
lives, our hopes, our spiritual journeys. Taylor became the
brother I never had.

Then very unexpectedly I got the news that Taylor had
dropped dead of a heart attack while he was out jogging.
He was only forty-two. Taylor's death consumed me with
grief. I cried. I questioned. At first, I could not think
beyond myself and my own pain. But then I began to feel
guilty for being so self-absorbed. After all, Taylor's wife
and children had lost even more than I had.

At the funeral, Taylor's family had the support of the
grieving community, which was as it should have been. But
because Taylor had meant so much to me, I wanted people
to tell me that they were sorry about my loss too. I wanted
to be comforted and consoled. I went through the service
and out to the cemetery feeling desolate and utterly alone in
my grief. At the gravesite, one of my clergy friends came
up and put his arm around me. "You and Taylor were good
friends, weren't you?" he said.

"Yes," I replied, "we were." That was all it took. With
my friend holding me in his arms and offering the comfort I
needed, sobs came from the depths of my heart.

Losing Taylor has given me a particular empathy for
others whose best friends die. Often the family of the
deceased doesn't know how close the friendship was.

Indeed, the family may not know it at all. This is particularly true when one befriends a co-worker or professional acquaintance and never thinks to mention it to the family.

Now when I preach at a funeral, I always remind myself to pay attention to the friends of the person who has died. Often I ask family members if they know who the best friends were. In some cases, I suggest that they invite these friends to a gathering where everyone can talk. I recall in particular the death of Arthur. As the family gathered to make funeral arrangements, Arthur's wife, Lucille, offhandedly mentioned that Billy was going to miss Arthur.

"Billy who?" I asked, knowing this was not one of the children's names.

"For years there was a family that lived down the street from us," Lucille explained. "Billy was their little boy. His dad died about five years ago, and Arthur took Billy under his wing. I guess you could say he became a second father to him."

Because of my experience with Taylor's death, I recognized the importance of including Billy in the funeral rites. He would need consolation and help in dealing with so important a loss in his life. The death of his surrogate father would probably cause him to relive the grief he felt when his own father died.

As Christians, we are called to reach out to those who are hurting, but it is unlikely that we would ever develop the compassion necessary for this work had we not at some time needed—and received—a helping hand ourselves. Through our own woundedness we arrive at our healing best.

My Road to Damascus

❧

A number of years ago I attended a
seminar on global issues ranging from nuclear war and
warming trends to population explosions and pollution. I
soon felt overwhelmed by the enormity of the problems and
my inability to do much of anything about them.

During a question-and-answer period, I expressed my
frustration, saying, "Sometimes I feel that all I can do is use
smaller-watt bulbs or go back to using the manual can
opener." The speaker's response proved to be a most
insightful gift both for my ministry and for helping others
discover theirs.

"What I suggest you do," the speaker said, "is pay
particular attention to the news for the next several days
and see what issue really grips you. See what angers or
saddens or frustrates you. Then formulate a plan and do
something *each week* to deal with that issue. For example,
if warming of the environment grabs you by the lapels,
spend fifteen minutes to half an hour each day just reading
about it. Do this until you feel well informed. Then join an
organization that deals with the problem, or support it
financially. If an ecological group is working to protect the
environment in your area, consider joining that."

The instant she said, "See what issue really grips you,"
the word *hunger* came to mind. World hunger was then,
and continues to be, an enormous problem. Although I
couldn't do anything on a grand scale, I could do
something. And I could do it in the area where I lived.

My commitment to the hunger issue led me to volunteer

at a soup kitchen one day each week. Some of the volunteers cook. Some set up the tables and chairs. Some clean up afterward. My job was to help serve the food. As the guests came through the line, I handed each one a bowl of soup and a sandwich.

One of the things I quickly discovered was that most of the guests were unwashed and they smelled really awful. To understand where I was coming from, you need to know that my mother was a nurse who had a real thing about cleanliness. During my childhood, she used to tell me to go outside and play but not get dirty. And she meant it! When I went through a push door, I was instructed to shove it with my fist. If the door had a handle, I was to pull it with my little finger. Either technique would limit the number of germs I got on my hands. Recently I was leaving an airport restroom and caught myself opening the door with my little finger. I laughed, thinking that at age forty-eight I probably had the strongest little finger in America.

Given my heightened awareness of germs, I made sure that I didn't touch the people coming through the line at the soup kitchen. This particular day we were serving chili and two pieces of buttered bread. The people thanked me as they took their food. Perhaps because I was wearing my clericals, some of them added, "Jesus loves you."

I noticed one man in the line who looked even more scruffy and broken than the others. When he got to me, I was overwhelmed by his stench. Like the pull of a magnet, my gaze went to the dirt and dried blood on his hands. Before I realized what was happening, he clasped my left hand in both of his. "Brother," he said, "I love you. Thanks for being here."

I swallowed hard before I could speak. "I'm glad you came," I said, trying to smile but not quite pulling it off.

"The Lord bless you." I handed him his food and he shuffled over to one of the tables.

The next man stepped up, and as I handed him his chili, a little spilled on my left hand. Instinctively, I licked it off. Then the shock of what I had done hit me. *That was the hand the man had just clasped!* I momentarily froze, repelled to think that I had licked something he had just touched.

Then all of a sudden the revulsion I felt dropped away and I sensed that I was on the Damascus Road. The light of awareness changed my vision and my heart warmed with new understanding. No longer was Jesus only the handsome man I had pictured in my mind and seen in paintings. Now he had a scarred, stubbled face and fingers stained yellow; he was dirty, he smelled bad, and he wore cast-off clothes. Jesus was one of the least of my brothers, and I had just served him chili and bread.

God's Yearning and Ours

Molly was an active, purposeful woman
in her forties who had been coming to see me on a regular
basis to talk about her spiritual formation. She wondered
how God was calling her to integrate her family and
professional life with her prayer life and ministry within the
church. One of the issues that had been puzzling Molly for
quite some time was what ministry she should become
involved in.

Using the advice I had been given at the seminar on
global issues, I said, "Why don't you take this month
between our meetings and really pay attention to the news.
See if there is any concern that grips you. Be alert for
anything that makes you especially angry or excites you.
When we get together again, we'll talk about your
experiences."

Another month passed. This time Molly arrived for our
meeting with a smile on her face. "Something quite
remarkable happened after our last meeting," she said.
"That very night, I spotted an article in the newspaper
about babies with AIDS. After I had read only a couple of
paragraphs, I was overwhelmed by a desire to do
something. At first I couldn't figure out where this great
rush of feeling came from, and then I remembered what
you said about the news and seeing if anything really
gripped me."

Molly went on to tell me how in the past month the topic
of AIDS leaped out at her no matter where she was —
visiting at a social gathering, watching TV, checking out at

the supermarket where magazines with articles about AIDS screamed for her attention. "This may be a silly comparison," she said, "but it was a little like what happens when you buy a red car. Suddenly you become aware of how many red cars are on the highway."

I nodded and asked what happened next.

With a satisfied sigh, Molly said, "I called and made arrangements to volunteer at a place where they need people to come and hold the babies with AIDS. We cuddle them and give them love. I have this deep-down feeling that this is work I am meant to do."

When people come seeking God's will for them in ministry, I share with them that the word *will,* which we translate from the Latin *voluntas,* means "yearning" in both Hebrew and Greek. To ask "What is God's *will* for me?" is the same as asking "What is God's *yearning* for me?" When Molly found a ministry that was just right for her, she satisfied the deep inner yearning that had been awakened by God's yearning for her.

In Search of the Answer

❧

I felt called to serve God long before I
was ordained. The big question for me was, In what
capacity? During that time of searching, I read books, took
courses, and talked with people I thought could be of help.
Friends who knew of my quest told me about Father P., a
professor from India who was said to be a wise spiritual
guide. As soon as I heard that he was living in Santa
Barbara, California, I knew I had to see him.

My job took me around the country, so when an
opportunity to fly to Los Angeles came along, I grabbed it.
In order to see Father P., I decided to take a day of my
vacation. I wrote for an appointment and his secretary
responded, saying that he could see me on the day I
suggested. I should arrive about four o'clock and plan to
stay for dinner. Needless to say, I was overjoyed.

Later in Los Angeles, I had a hard time keeping my
mind on business. All I thought about was the upcoming
meeting with the one who would surely have The
Answer. When my work in L.A. was finished, I rented a
car and made the hundred-plus-mile drive north. After
wending my way through the foothills of Santa Barbara,
I found the house. It was a magnificent place complete
with a pristine blue swimming pool and a stunning view
of the mountains. I rang the bell and a young man, whom
I later learned came from east India, opened the door.

"Hello," he said in a thin, unsure voice. "You here to
see Father?"

"Yes. I'm Ron DelBene from Florida."

"You come in. I not speak much English." I followed him into the living room where he motioned me to sit. "Father not here. Be back later."

My stand-in host was a visitor who, indeed, spoke very little English. I didn't speak a word of his language, so we gestured and nodded a lot. After a prolonged exchange of pleasantries that lapsed into an awkward silence, he got me a drink.

A half hour crept by.

Then an hour.

The longer I waited, the more annoyed I became. *Who does this Father P. think he is?* I huffed to myself. *Doesn't he know I'm a national consultant in religion and that my time is important? After I've made such an effort to be here, he should be able to keep his appointment!*

At five-thirty — an hour and a half after I arrived — Father P. whisked into the room. I don't know which was greater, my anger or my disappointment. This short, slightly built person didn't look at all like the wise man I had pictured. He didn't even have a beard! "I am sorry to be late," he said. "I did not have any way to be in touch with you. I hope you enjoyed visiting with my friend."

"It was an experience," I murmured.

"Come into my office." I followed him into his library, a huge room with two walls of windows. He sat behind a massive oak desk and motioned me to a chair opposite him. "Now," he said, "tell me why you have come to see me."

By this time my anger had evaporated and I had forgotten my disappointment. For more than an hour I opened myself up to him. It was as if he had turned on a tap and out gushed my hopes, fears, anxieties, dreams. When I was finished, Father P. nodded reflectively. Then he scurried from behind his desk, pulled up a chair, and sat so close that our knees touched. "Now," he directed, "pay attention!"

I was certain he was going to place his hands on my head, or my heart, and that I would explode in ecstasy. This wise man held the key to meaning and purpose in my life. With him lay the answers. My heart thumped with anticipation as he looked me straight in the eye. This is what I had come for. This was my moment of truth.

Father P. had no lead-in, no preliminaries. In his rapid-fire voice, he simply rattled off three things I must do. Then he dusted his hands in a kind of case dismissed gesture and stood up. "Let's go eat," he said, and he was out the door before I had a chance to respond. As I followed him to the table, I thought, *I came all the way from Florida for this?* The air had been let out of my balloon. Deflated and disillusioned, I sat through dinner with little interest in the food or the conversation.

When I got home to Florida, Eleanor was naturally curious about my meeting with the Wise One. We sat facing each other and I told her the whole story, down to the smallest detail. She was totally absorbed. When I got to the part about Father P. looking me square in the eye, she leaned forward. "He told me," I said with the hush of confidentiality, "that there are three things I must do: One, pray unceasingly. Two, go home and love my wife and children. Three, do what needs to be done."

Eleanor's gaze held fast to mine as she said, "Thank God, someone finally told you that!"

Over the years I have shared this story many times with people who come to me seeking to know God's yearning for themselves. I find that the three things I was told can, with a bit of adaptation, be applied to anyone's life. In retrospect, Father P. was a far wiser man than I appreciated at the time.

Connecting with Scripture

One Sunday when the readings were
about Ezekiel, I preached a sermon on dreams and
expressed my belief that often in dreams the spirit of God
breaks through into our consciousness. After the service, a
parishioner I had always perceived as a staid and
conservative professional came up to me. "Do you do a lot
of work with dreams?" he asked. There was a warmth
about him that I had never detected before.

I told him that I had done some studying on the subject
and again remarked about the number of times dreams are
mentioned in the scripture. I wanted to make sure he
didn't think this was just some trendy thing to be into, but
that throughout history God has used dreams to speak to
us.

He nodded, shook my hand, and said, "Maybe I'll give
you a call. I'd like to talk about a recurring dream I've been
having."

Later he did call, and as soon as he walked into my
office he got right to the point. "For several years I've been
having this dream, and the scene is always the same. A
huge eagle is sitting on a high rock. It sits for awhile and
then flies away. That's it! That's the dream."

"What does the dream mean to you?" I asked. We talked
about some ideas he had, and I said, "Can you think of any
scripture that mentions a rock?"

He thought for a minute and then mentioned Peter whose
name means *rock*. He also recalled the admonition not to
build a house on sand but instead to build it on rock. When

I asked about the eagle, he was stumped. Shaking his head, he said, "Nothing comes to mind."

I went to my desk and got a Bible dictionary. Opening it to the word *eagle*, I showed him the many places in scripture where the word is used. Then I did the same for *rock*. "Why don't you take this dictionary with you and look up the scripture references," I suggested. "See if you get any insights into your dreams. You might want to keep a journal."

"I'll do that," he said, and our meeting ended.

The next week he was brisk and businesslike as usual, only this time he was obviously excited. "My search this week was quite an experience," he said, and right away started to share some insights. "I'm an attorney and I spend a lot of time looking at contracts. I look for certain words and loopholes that are clues to understanding the whole contract. Using the Bible dictionary is a lot like that."

This was but one of many instances that have made me aware of how gracious God is to call us right where we are to use the tools at hand. So simple a thing as introducing a man to a Bible dictionary helped him connect with scripture in a way that suited his intellectual approach to matters and meshed with his professional training.

Putting on Christ

❧

For almost six years Dale came to see
me once a month for spiritual direction. During that time,
he moved through exciting adventures with God that
influenced every aspect of his life. One fall he was
diagnosed with cancer.

As the disease progressed, Dale and I talked about the
issues one faces when death is imminent: finances, funeral
arrangements, leave-taking. One of our visits during his
final weeks took place at his home. He was still working as
an ophthalmologist for a while in the morning, coming
home to rest and then going back to the office in the
afternoon. On this particular day, he was lying on his bed
resting and we were talking about what the next life would
be like. He spoke of his grief at leaving his wife, children,
and friends, yet he looked forward to being reunited with
young Dale, his son who had died some years before. Then
getting off the bed, he eased into a chair and we sat face-to-
face. From out of nowhere, Dale asked, "What size suit do
you wear, Ron?"

"Forty regular."

"Would you mind wearing someone else's clothes?"

"No. Why?"

"Because after I'm dead, you're going to have some nice
clothes." With great effort, Dale got up and walked over to
his closet. Pulling out sleeves of his suits and jackets, he
reminded me of a salesperson as he said, "You'll look good
in this . . . This is a good color . . . this is a wonderful
fabric." Then he pulled out a gray herringbone sportcoat.

"When you wear this, I want you to remember that it was my favorite."

Dale had always stood out as being especially well dressed and now *he was leaving his clothes to me*! I stood there stunned and groped for words to express my feelings. Already grieving the loss of this good and kind friend, all I could manage to say was, "Thank you so much, Dale. I'm touched and honored."

Dale dismissed my gratitude with a wave of his hand. "What size shoe do you wear?"

"Nine and a half . . . or ten."

"Can't help you there. I'm an eight and a half."

"Tell you what," I said, "you provide the suits and I'll provide the shoes." We laughed together for what turned out to be the last time.

The following week was Holy Week. Saddened as I was at the prospect of losing a friend, Dale's gift helped me find new meaning in the death and resurrection of Jesus.

One problem I've always had with the death of Jesus— and I suspect this is true for a lot of Christians—is that it doesn't seem real. When I was in Nicaragua and listened to some of the mothers who had seen their sons and daughters killed, I got physically ill just hearing about the barbarity. Yet I can conduct a Holy Week service in which the passion of our Lord Jesus Christ is read and I am not deeply affected. Perhaps this is because the crucifixion happened some 2,000 years ago and time has distanced us from it emotionally. After my experience in Nicaragua, I decided that each Holy Week I was going to look for a symbol or image that spoke to me in a personal way about Jesus' death and resurrection. This year Dale's gift provided me with what I was looking for.

Five days after my last visit with Dale, I preached at a

small celebration of the Eucharist during Holy Week. After telling about my friendship with Dale and the gift of his clothes, I said, "When I put on one of Dale's jackets or a pair of his slacks, I'm going to remember that he was a gracious, gentle man who loved his family and was loyal to his friends. I'm going to recall that he was honorable in all his dealings and dedicated himself to working for social justice. I'll also remember that he suffered a painful death and now lives a new, risen life. What is true of Dale is also true of Jesus. I believe that Dale's life serves as an example of what it means to put on the mind of Christ." I concluded by saying, "Each time I put on Dale's clothing, I will remind myself to also put on Christ—to live as he did and to do as he did. Dale's life, death, and passage to risen life will be a symbol for me of the death and resurrection of Jesus."

Dale died shortly after Easter, and I later received his clothing. Since then I've worn something of his nearly every day. And when I do, I remember.

We Never Walk Alone

Young children who are trying hard to be independent and establish their own identity like to say, "I did it all myself." But as we become adults—and if we are honest with ourselves—we realize that there is little if anything we actually do all by ourselves.

When several of our seminary graduates were being ordained, I wrote to each of them, passing on some advice I was given a long time ago. "Make a list of all the people who have been significant to you, who have formed your character and helped you get where you are," I told them. I knew they would think of parents and other relatives, friends and coaches, ministers and favorite teachers, and all those who had nurtured them with love and encouragement. But I also told them to think of those people who, though they might not bring back fond memories, played important roles in their lives. Was there a teacher who was a particularly hard taskmaster? A neighbor who called them to account? A mentor who told them what they needed to know instead of what they wanted to hear?

I suggested to these seminarians that they put their lists in an accessible place and add to them as other names came to mind. "Prior to your ordination," I wrote in my letter to them, "put the names on a 3" x 5" card. Sometime during the ceremony, take the card out and read the names to yourself. Let this be a reminder that as you move forward to be ordained, you are not walking alone. All those people on your list are walking with you."

I also suggest to engaged couples that they make such a list before they get married. Doing so helps them see the part others have played in their achievements and blessings. What I have done in my own life is to keep my list in the back of my journal. Every time I move to a new journal I copy the list. At least, that's what I did until I began journaling on a computer. Now I call up my list periodically, review it, and perhaps add a name or two. Many of the people on my list have died, but because they once walked with me, I believe they continue to do so as they live on in risen life. I find life to be more of a joy knowing that I do not walk alone.

God, Break the Teeth
in Their Mouths

So often I encounter people who have
been taught that it's wrong to be angry or jealous or
resentful. Because they aren't supposed to experience these
feelings, they shut down all their emotions. One important
aspect of ministry is helping people get in touch with what
they are feeling.

I received a call one Monday morning from a very angry
parishioner. In a crisp voice, Suzanne said, "I have to see
you today." I set up an appointment for eleven-thirty and
precisely on time, Suzanne strode into my office with her
teeth clenched and a scowl on her face. I invited her to sit
down and asked her what was going on.

Suzanne explained that the past Friday evening her son,
Brett, and his friends had been at a basketball game where
some rowdiness had broken out. Brett was identified as one
of the instigators. He confessed to being involved, but other
boys—who were every bit as involved as he was—got
away. That morning Suzanne learned that the principal had
suspended Brett.

"Brett is very upset by the unfairness of the whole
thing," Suzanne remarked. "After the suspension, he said,
'I wish lightning would strike down that principal!' I told
him he shouldn't feel that way, yet those are my feelings
exactly and I feel guilty for having them."

I gestured her to stop for a moment. Taking my Bible, I
opened it to Psalm 58 and read: "O God, break the teeth in

their mouths. . . . Let them vanish like water that runs away; like grass let them be trodden down and wither" (verses 6, 7; RSV).

"Those are my feelings exactly!" Suzanne interrupted, a look of astonishment on her face. "You mean someone in the Bible actually *admitted* to feeling that way?"

"Yes, indeed!" I assured her, and we both laughed. I went on to explain that reading the psalms is like reading other people's journals. We peer over the writers' shoulders and see how they speak to God. What we discover is that they don't just talk about love and gratitude. They talk about being scared and angry and vengeful. The great message of the psalms is that all is known before God, so verbalizing our thoughts and feelings is the beginning of moving into greater wholeness and growth.

After we visited a while longer, Suzanne left feeling a good deal calmer than when she arrived. I hope she understood that it's good to get troubling feelings out in the open where they can be examined and then dealt with in a positive way. I frequently use the psalms as examples of people getting in touch with their feelings and then discovering that God is there for them in ways they have never before experienced.

Remember the Fisherfolk

❧

Have you ever been in a situation in

which you unwittingly demanded that people walk with you but they kept dragging their feet? It happened to me in a small parish where I was serving in the early eighties. The Christian singing group The Fisherfolk was very popular at the time. I knew several people in the group, and at various conferences we shared many special times together. Because I was such a fan of The Fisherfolk style of singing, I tried teaching my parishioners the songs the group had popularized.

Although we sang the songs week after week, my enthusiasm for the music didn't catch on. No matter how hard I tried, I couldn't ignite the spark that got the congregation singing with gusto. One day I mentioned this to the music director. "Something's just not right, Sharon," I said. "We're making a pass at the songs, but we're not pulling them off."

Sharon didn't respond right away. She seemed to be weighing how forthright she dared be. "Well," she finally said, "what I think is happening when we sing these songs is that we're singing with you and you're singing with The Fisherfolk."

It took a few moments for me to fully comprehend what Sharon was saying. Then I laughed. "You're absolutely right," I told her. "Whenever we sing those songs— especially my favorites—I'm not in church, at least not in my mind. Instead, I'm back at the base of the Rockies or in North Carolina marching around the campfire and singing to the strum of guitars."

Sharon made some suggestions about church music. When we picked up on her ideas, the singing took on new vitality. As for me, whenever I find myself trying to pull people along and their reluctance is obvious, I say to myself, "Okay, DelBene, remember The Fisherfolk."

Love Hits Hard

❧

One fall during my years in campus

ministry, a student who was struggling to find his way in college came to see me. Brian and I discussed issues he had in common with other young men and women away from home for the first time: handling independence, examining values, relationships with friends and family. In one particularly touching session, I discovered that Brian had a deep yearning for his dad's affection. As we ended our time together, I reached out and put my hand on his shoulder. Brian flinched, then lowered his head and arched his back a bit.

Brian's instinctive reaction triggered questions for me. "Let's sit back down a minute," I said. "There's something I want to ask you."

Brian was over six feet tall, but the first time I met him, I noticed that he hunched his shoulders upward and thrust his head forward. I thought that his rather odd posture might be due to some discomfort he felt about being tall. But now I had another idea. "Brian," I said, "how did your father show affection to you? Did he ever say, 'You've done a good job, Son'?"

Brian nodded. "Oh, yeah. Many times."

"Did he do anything when he said it? Did he put his arm around your shoulder or give you a hug?"

Brian frowned. "My dad had a habit of walking up behind me and swatting me on the back of the head. 'Good boy, Brian,' he'd say, 'I'm proud of you.'"

Now the pieces fit together. "Brian, are you aware that

you flinched when I reached out to put my hand on your shoulder?"

"Yeah."

"Did you expect me to hit you?"

"I guess so." Brian's eyes widened as he realized what I was getting at. "That's what my dad always did, wasn't it? He was trying to tell me he loved me, but he was hitting me instead."

I tell Brian's story as a reminder that our bodies and our emotions are connected in intricate and fascinating ways. An awareness of this connection keeps us sensitive to behavior that opens doors to new insights into our own lives and into the lives of others as well.

Freeing the Tears

Dorothy was a single woman in her
forties who had been physically abused as a child. After
about a year of spiritual direction with me, she reserved
eight days at The Hermitage—a small place of retreat that
Eleanor and I have on our property. Not uncommonly,
people who spend time in solitude and prayer find that
revealing dreams surface. One morning when I went out to
see Dorothy, she mentioned a troubling dream she had had
the night before. "I'm quite certain it's a remembrance,"
she said, "because I woke up in a panic state."

In her dream, Dorothy was about five years old. Her dad
had torn off her blouse and thrown her on the bed. "He was
beating my bare back with a belt," she said. "My back was
bleeding; and every time I cried, he beat me harder. Then I
heard him leave the room. I had the strange feeling that I
was in the dream, and yet I wasn't because I was watching
what was happening. When he came back, he had a salt
shaker and proceeded to rub salt in the cuts on my back."

The horror of what that little child had endured brought
tears to my eyes. But Dorothy was dry-eyed, and with no trace
of emotion went on with her story. "Right then I remember
saying *'I will not cry.'* You know, Ron, we've talked about the
fact that I don't ever in my entire lifetime remember crying. I
know there are gallons of tears bottled up inside me, but I
can't get the lid off. I just can't let the tears out."

We sat in silence for quite some time before Dorothy
said, "Where was God in all this? Why would God let such
a thing happen?"

"I don't know why you had to endure those beatings, Dorothy," I responded gently. "But I believe that God is bringing these memories to your conscious mind so that you can embrace and heal the child within you." I suggested that she sit in prayer that afternoon and place herself back in the situation. "When you are there, look for Jesus. Perhaps he will already be present, or at some point he may appear."

That evening I went back to The Hermitage. When I saw the peaceful expression on Dorothy's face, I knew that something extraordinary had happened.

Dorothy explained that she had put herself back in the situation as I suggested and had asked God to be with her. "After the beating ended, I was sitting on the edge of the bed," she said. "I just sat there staring into space and refusing to cry. Then I found myself whispering, 'Jesus, Jesus.' Suddenly he was there, standing right in front of me. 'Why did you let him do that to me? I demanded. Why didn't you stop him?' With a look of tenderness that I will never forget, Jesus reached out and touched my head. 'Dorothy,' he said, 'I know what it is to be beaten. I am with you.'" Dorothy paused as if to recapture the sacredness of her experience. "In that moment, all the power the beatings had over me evaporated."

"Dorothy," I said, "it's time to embrace who you are. Can you say, 'My name is Dorothy, and I am an abused child'"?

She looked at me, startled. "I don't know."

"I believe you can. And it's time to do it. It's time to stand before God as that abused child."

Looking at me straight in the eye, she said, "My name is Dorothy . . . and ah . . . uh. . . ." The words stuck in her throat.

"You can do it, Dorothy," I urged. "You can say the words."

She tried again in a quivering voice. "I am Dorothy and . . . uh . . ." Then in a forceful spurt came the words, "I am an abused child." With that, Dorothy began to weep. She put her head on the table and sobbed from the very depths of her soul.

I placed my hands on her head. "You are being healed, Dorothy. These are the tears of a lifetime. Let them flow so the healing continues and you can be free of the oppression of abuse in your past."

I often share Dorothy's story with adults who were abused children. As pastors we are graced with opportunities to walk with our people through the deaths and resurrections in their lives. Anytime a broken life is made whole, anytime old hurts are healed and despair turns to hope or hate turns to love, we witness the rebirth of the human spirit. Sometimes in our ministries we meet a Dorothy and are privileged to play a part in a resurrection that might not have happened had we not been there with them as a vehicle of God's healing.

Saints in the Making

A priest friend who had done a good
job of pastoring over the years came to The Hermitage to
spend a week on retreat. Joel was in his late fifties, married
with grown children and anticipating a soon-to-be-born
grandchild. On the first night of his stay, we spent time
talking about why he had come and what his expectations
were for this time of reflection and prayer.

With a sigh of frustration, he said, "You know, Ron,
when I was a young man, I felt that God called me in a
special way and I wanted to be a saint. So I went to
seminary and found that all they do is make priests. Now
I've been a priest for more than twenty-five years and I still
want to be a saint."

*Is Joel chasing the impossible dream? Or can one be a
saint in today's world?* We talked about what it means to be
a saint—how each person seems to have a different
definition and how our religious culture has made a saint
into almost mythic proportions. As we reflected, I shared
with him one definition I especially like: "Saints are people
who make it easier for others to believe in God." So how
does a person become one of those special people?

Over the years I, too, have tried many ways to be a saint
and for a long time thought that the more difficult the
approach the more worth it would have. The longer I live
and the more I share with others about their spiritual
journeys, the more clearly I see that the way to become a
saint is simply to live the two commandments Jesus gave
us: First to love God with your whole heart and soul and

mind and second to love your neighbor as yourself (Matt. 22:37, AP).

Sainthood does not require that we go off to a monastery or become a hermit. Love can be lived out wherever we are and in whatever our circumstances. So why aren't there more saints among us? Perhaps it's because living a life of love isn't easy. It demands that we be attentive to our inner spiritual life and intentional about our justice ministry with all of God's people. And when we fail in love, as we often do, God asks that we try again with renewed effort. From what I know of Joel, that's pretty much how he lives his life. So maybe he's a saint in the making. And maybe you and I are too.

Christy with Them

In the early spring of 1985, I traveled

to Nicaragua with a delegation of twenty-five other
Americans from various religious backgrounds. The trip
was part of my church's ministry to support peace and
justice throughout the world. Upon our return we prepared
a report that was delivered to Congress.

I had long anticipated visiting the cathedral in Managua.
For many years it had stood in the center of the city as the
proud accomplishment of a faith-filled people. But when at
last I walked into this once majestic structure, my heart
lurched. The cathedral, like the country, was a scene of
destruction. The roof was gone and a thick layer of hard-
packed dirt covered the floor. In any cathedral, the eye is
drawn to the high altar. But here the huge marble slab that
had served as the Lord's Table lay across the steps about
fifteen feet away, where the earthquake of 1972 had thrown it.

Everything of value in the cathedral had been stripped
away, including the tabernacle that fit into a niche in the
center of the high altar. All that remained was the
indentation where the golden box containing the blessed
bread and wine had been. Printed on the back panel of the
indentation were the words *Cristo Vive, Cristo Viene
Pronto (Christ is alive, Christ is coming soon)*. Scrawled
between these two declarations was the word *Presente*.
This proclaimed Christ as the first and central martyr
among us.

I thought of the first Easter morning when from inside
the tomb the messenger said, "Why are you looking among

the dead for one who is alive? He is not here; he has been raised" (Luke 24:5 TEV). In this country where the land had been so scarred and the people had suffered so greatly, the belief still prevailed that Christ was with them. Hope was still alive.

¡Presente!

❧

On a Thursday a young man from the

Nicaraguan congregation we were visiting was killed by
the Contras. Now it was Sunday and the Eucharist was his
memorial. Questions and conflicting thoughts filled my
mind. Would that young man have been killed if my
government had not been supporting the Contras? What
does it mean when a mother who sits two pews ahead of
me says that the blood of her dead son is the blood of
freedom for the people? When that young man and two
others from the parish are called martyrs, why are my
feelings of sorrow tinged with confusion?

From the altar the priest says, "The peace of the Lord be
with you." While I am trying to sort through the tangle of
my thoughts, people for whom war is a way of life
embrace me and say, *"Paz."*

During the Eucharist there is a pause and the
congregation is silent. Then someone calls out a name. In
one voice everyone responds, *"¡Presente!"*

Another name is called out. Again all respond,
"¡Presente!"

At least twenty names are called out and each time the
response is the same: *"¡Presente!"*

I didn't fully understand what was happening until I
heard the name "Oscar Romero." Then I knew that the
names were of those persons who had died, and I joined in
shouting *"¡PRESENTE!"*

Presente is used by school children to answer roll call.
But the word has other meanings that are more difficult to

define. At the Eucharist, *presente* means "in our midst" or "present with us." It is a way of proclaiming the reality of the communion of saints.

I recalled the woman at the beginning of the service referring to the dead as martyrs of Christ for freedom. Were we then celebrating the Eucharist over the bones of martyrs? I began to understand in a new way the ancient custom of placing the bones of martyrs in the altar. These relics made the martyrs present to us just as the dead victims are present when their names are called out.

As the memorial came to a close, Padre Molina said to the congregation, "Now let us stand and share a song to show our solidarity with our brothers and sisters from North America." (And I thought we had come to show our solidarity with *them*!) The musicians played the melody and we all joined hands. In English, the congregation began singing "We Shall Overcome," the song that has become the rallying cry for the oppressed.

Time collapsed and memories flooded back. Oppression is oppression whether it is in our own country or in another part of the world. The names of the countries change, but the questions remain the same: Who is the enemy? What is the truth? The answers are debatable, but as long as tyranny exists and people are suffering, God's reign is not totally present and we who call ourselves Christ's followers have work to do.

The Same Good News

As I entered the church of Saint Mary of the Angels in one of Managua's barrios, I saw my stole. Well, not actually *my* stole, but the priest behind the altar was wearing a stole identical to one I often wore back home. His had the same colors, the same designs. Both had been woven by Indians in Guatemala.

I have stoles from many different parts of the world: Niger, Greece, Mexico, and Ghana, to name a few. When I celebrate the Eucharist wearing a stole from a distant place, I experience a deep sense of oneness with people whose customs and language are different from mine but who share a common faith.

Seeing a stole like mine being worn by someone about to celebrate the Eucharist reminded me that all of us who stand around the Lord's Table and profess a faith in Jesus are family. When we put on the stole, we become more than just ourselves. We become a corporate person who symbolizes what Jesus came to teach. The country and the faces change and the language may be different from the one we speak, but whether being preached in Managua, Nicaragua, or Alabama, the Good News remains the same.

Could a Loving Father Do Such a Thing?

The topic of my talk had been "Living into Prayer." Some of the people who heard it wanted to explore the subject further and I agreed to stay after the session and meet with them. Nine of us circled our chairs in a corner of the conference room.

Sitting to my left was Marcie, a deacon in her church who was coming up for elder's orders and finding it hard to pray. "I'm really under a lot of stress right now," she said. "I'm ready to go up for my interview, and this will be my second time. The first time I was told I needed more work on my Christology, especially the redemption of Jesus." She looked at me as though hopeful I might be able to help. "You know, Ron, I have a hard time understanding how a good God—a God whom Jesus called Father—could give his son over to be crucified. We say it's so wonderful that God did this, but I just can't accept that. Something isn't right."

From an earlier discussion with Marcie, I suspected that she had been abused as a child. "I'm beginning to believe more and more in the importance of our childhood experiences to our theological development," I said. "Especially our experiences within the family. For example, I've discovered that those who have experienced abuse from a parent often find it difficult to deal with certain theological positions—"

"My God!" she interrupted, her words exploding like a

cork from a bottle. "I was sexually abused by my father when I was a little girl."

In the silence that followed I could hear my own breathing. This woman, who was now in her mid-thirties, had unlocked a secret door in her life, and the rest of us were left to imagine all the pain inherent in her experience. The compassion and tenderness of the group were palpable, and I knew that we were on holy ground.

I went on to say "A sexually abusive parent typically says 'I really love you. What we're doing is special between us.' Yet at the same time the child feels guilty and knows something is wrong. Things just don't quite fit together."

Marcie nodded. "That's it exactly."

Again there was a long silence. This time it was broken by a gray-haired man in shirt-sleeves. "I too was sexually abused by my father," he said in a voice husky with emotion. "And during all these years of my ministry, I have never been able to preach on Good Friday. I have never been able to believe that God, the loving Father, could let his son be crucified."

The ensuing conversation was a deeply moving and tender exploration of how we come to God in unique ways. I was aware that we were all awed by how gracious God is to love us unconditionally. When the group dispersed, I went to my room with a sorrowing but grateful heart: sorrowing that adults can inflict such pain on their children and grateful that two people had found a safe place to share their secret shame. I later learned that the elderly pastor was on Marcie's interview committee. When she came before the committee this time, his response to her was certain to be tempered with new understanding.

The Investment of Talents

Bert was a short, mild-mannered man

who typically wore dark-blue work pants and a white shirt with the sleeves rolled up. Although he attended church regularly, I rarely saw him in a suit. And, of course, never a tie. When I was first introduced to Bert, he hung back a bit as though intimidated by being around a minister.

Bert was known around church as the guy who could fix anything. I never sought his mechanical expertise until my balky old car got harder and harder to start. It had been in the shop several times, and Bert was my last hope that the problem could be found and corrected.

I had hardly put the phone down before Bert wheeled into the driveway in a black pickup that looked like one of Henry Ford's originals. Not one for small talk, he went right to work under the hood. He tinkered a while and pretty soon hollered, "I see what it is! Get in and start 'er up!" I did as he said and the engine kicked in right away.

"Turn 'er off!" Bert yelled.

I got out of the car and went around to where Bert was working. "All I know about a car is where to put the gas," I admitted. "I'm not even sure I can tell you where the spark plugs are. But you come along and spot the problem right away. It makes me feel like a dummy."

Bert slowly pulled back from beneath the hood. With a wrench in one hand and his head cocked to the left, he drawled, "If I had to stand up in front of everybody in church and preach, I'd pass out!"

"Well, Bert, I guess we all have our talents."

He nodded. "Guess so."

Bert was never one to consult me about anything personal, so I knew something was up the day he came to the church to see me. I invited him into my office, which was a converted storage room that was so small we sat knee to knee. Holding his head down and avoiding eye contact, Bert told me how dissatisfied he was with his job: He didn't like it. He saw no future in it. He wanted out but wasn't sure what moves to make.

"Have you ever dreamed about something you'd like to do, Bert?" I asked.

Without a moment's hesitation, he replied, "Always dreamed I'd like to own my own business."

We talked for about half an hour more before I said, "You know, Bert, maybe it's time to go for your dream. Why not try some other line of work for awhile? See what else you can do and what doors open up."

Not long after that, Bert heard of a small machine shop about sixty miles away whose owner was looking for help. Bert quit his old job and began commuting to work. After about a year and a half, the owner asked Bert if he wanted to buy the business.

That is in fact what Bert did; and as the eighties came to a close, his business netted more than he ever thought possible. Bert now has several employees and looks forward to getting up each day and going to work. But other things about his life haven't changed. He still doesn't feel real comfortable wearing a suit, and he's as unassuming as ever about his talents.

In Frederick's Place

In every parish there seems to be at least

one person who is a major pain. Frederick was that pain for
me. Always critical. Always opinionated. Always right.
And as is the habit of most of the Fredericks in our
churches, he always came to the same service and sat in the
same pew in exactly the same spot. I talked with my
spiritual director about how annoying I found Frederick to
be, and he suggested that I pray for him daily. Wise person
that he is, my spiritual director knows that our feelings
often change when we hold someone in our mind and heart
in daily prayer.

In my office at church, I had set aside a special place to
pray. That is where I remembered Frederick each day.
Meanwhile, I began reading some retreat talks by Evelyn
Underhill, the well-known writer and spiritual guide. In one
of her talks given to clergy in the 1920s Underhill
expressed amazement at how few clergy pray in their
churches. Upon examining my own prayer practices, I
realized that I usually prayed in church only as part of
worship services. Right then I decided to try praying there
at other times as well.

At first, I prayed in the sanctuary. Sitting in a chair that
I used on Sunday, I faithfully remembered Frederick.
Then one day as I walked into the church, my gaze
unaccountably fixed itself on the pew where Frederick sat
week in and week out. I felt drawn to his pew, so instead
of going to my usual place near the altar, I sat in
Frederick's place.

That was Tuesday and I decided to sit there during my prayer time for the rest of the week. In the beginning my prayers for Frederick flowed pretty well. I asked God's blessing on every aspect of his life. But on Friday my wellspring dried up. No matter how deep I plumbed, no prayer came forth. So instead of trying to pray verbally, I simply sat in the empty church, absorbing the silence and being attentive to God's presence. After a time, a profound sense of peace came over me. I felt no need to pray for anyone or anything. It was as if the Spirit wanted me to understand that with God there is no us and them, no yours and mine. With God we are all one. As I have come to comprehend this connectedness we have with one another, the Fredericks in my life have become far less troubling.

In the years since then, I have made it a practice to pray in the worship space of the churches I serve. I always pick a different place to sit. Often it is a place where someone I know sits each week. When I get up in front of the congregation on Sunday, I see myself sitting all around the church and am reminded that in the great mystery of God's love we are all united.

And Ain't It a Blessing!

My week had been especially hectic.

After three evening meetings in a row, I had to get up at five
to make it to a six-thirty class at the church. Although I
enjoyed teaching the class, I was tired even before I started
the day. As I pulled into my parking space, a woman was
cutting across the church lot. Given the earliness of the hour
and the neighborhood toward which she was headed, I
imagined she was a maid on her way to work. On this brisk
February morning she wore a plaid knit hat topped by a large
pom-pom and had a wool scarf tied under her coat collar.

As I opened my car door, our eyes met. Stifling a yawn, I
said, "Another day, another dollar."

She broke stride momentarily; and a smile, warm and
bright as spring sunshine, lit her face. With a lilt in her
voice she said, "And ain't it a blessing!"

For a few moments I watched as she went her way, the
pom-pom bobbing jauntily. She had probably gotten up an
hour before I had, ridden a bus downtown, and transferred
to a second bus to reach this neighborhood, where she
would spend her day looking after other people's children
or cleaning another family's house. Yet she saw the day as
a blessing and I—who so often referred to myself as a
servant to the congregation—saw it as a grind.

When I got out of the car, I filled my lungs with the crisp
air and looked to the east, where the sun was just beginning
to brighten the sky. "This is the day the Lord has made," I
said to myself. And a woman whose name I did not know
had reminded me to rejoice and be glad in it.

Led by a Little Child

I went to Namibia in the fall of 1986 to visit parishes there and help conduct a clergy conference. One Sunday I stood outside a little tin-roofed church in the war-torn north greeting people as they arrived for the service. A man approached, holding the hand of a delicate-looking girl of about three wearing a pink dress trimmed in white lace. As I welcomed him, the little girl he introduced as his daughter shrank back, watching me warily. The father nudged her forward, wanting her to meet the white priest who had come 880 kilometers into the bush country to preach and celebrate the Eucharist.

"Walelepo—Good Morning!" I said to the child in what I hoped was a kindly voice. I squatted to be closer to her height and tried to put her at ease. But when I offered my hand, she bolted back against the security of her father's leg. Her eyes were wide with fear.

The father gently took his daughter's hand and extended it toward mine. "Sometimes she be a little afraid because you are like men who come to torture us last weeks," he said apologetically.

Much as I wanted to say something comforting, I simply had no words adequate to express my sorrow and regret at what this man and his people had endured—and would perhaps endure in the future. As I released the little girl's hand, I heard in my head the words *and a little child will lead them.* But what did this mean in my life? Where was this child leading me?

Since being in Namibia, I have been led to a deeper appreciation of the strength of the human spirit. I have come to see that many people survive even the harshest of cruelties and do not give up on life. They retain their capacity to love and even dare to hope that they will find love in return. Surely this kind of strength has to come from God who is present with us in suffering and who gives us faith enough to keep on believing that justice and kindness will prevail.

Free at Last

❧

I first met Elizabeth when her husband,

Jim, was dying of a lingering illness. Over time we became friends. I was there for her when Jim died and later shared in her grief. A few years after Jim's death, Elizabeth had her own health problems. She suffered a heart attack and kidney failure and was in a lot of pain. On more than one of my visits, she asked, "Why is God punishing me?"

I responded that I don't believe God uses sickness as a punishment but that it is common for people who are ill to look back at their lives in search of a reason for their pain. We spent a good deal of time talking about how God is present for us in our suffering and gives us the strength to bear our pain, even though we may not always feel that presence. I suggested to Elizabeth that she might find comfort in uniting her pain with others who are suffering. This is especially helpful when the suffering person has someone specific in mind. Thinking of another hurting person keeps patients mindful that they are not alone; suffering is shared by many.

Still, Elizabeth persisted in thinking of her health problems as a punishment. One day when she again asked, "Why is God punishing me?" I said almost without thinking, "Why do you feel that God is punishing you?"

Immediately she replied, "Because I prayed for Jim to die."

A light snapped on in my head. I had been treating Elizabeth's question as theological, but she was trying to deal with guilt feelings that had probably been troubling her ever since her husband's death.

"You think God is punishing you because you prayed for Jim to die," I repeated.

"Yes," she said just above a whisper. "He wanted to die, you know. He was so tired of illness and pain. He kept saying to me 'Why don't I die?' And I prayed that he would. It wasn't just a few prayers either. For a long time I prayed that he would die. When he finally did, I was so thankful that he didn't have to suffer anymore. But then I began feeling guilty."

I recalled that following Jim's death, Elizabeth mentioned feeling guilty because she was free. He was no longer on her mind constantly. She could relax and go places with friends. With only herself to think about, there was a carefree quality to her life.

I moved my chair closer to Elizabeth's bed and took her hand. "Elizabeth," I said, "in my many years of ministering to people with terminally ill loved ones, I have found that at some point virtually all of them pray for that loved one to die."

Elizabeth turned her head on the pillow and looked into my eyes. "Really? I thought I was the only one."

"No, you are not alone," I assured her. "You are in the company of a lot of people who want what is best for someone they love. Have you ever thought that your prayers for Jim might have been the same as those of Mary and the friends of Jesus who stood beneath the cross and watched him slowly die? Praying for someone's suffering to end unites you with a great many others."

We talked a while longer, and before I left we prayed together. Then making the sign of the cross on her forehead, I said, "Elizabeth, you are now truly free."

"Thank you," she murmured. "Thank you so much."
That evening Elizabeth died.

He Touched Me

Each Wednesday our church holds a

mid-morning Eucharist. One morning as I greeted people before the service, a parishioner told me that she had just come from visiting her mother in the nursing home. Even if she hadn't mentioned the visit I would have known because my nose had picked up the scent of antiseptic cleanliness— a smell so pervasive in some care facilities that it clings to the clothes of visitors.

The smell triggered memories of my grandfather and visits to the nursing home where he spent the final years of his life. As the service began, my personal remembrances gave way to thoughts of people from the parish who were in hospitals or care facilities. During the first two scripture readings and the psalm, I recalled the parishioners individually and briefly prayed for each. Then it was time for me to read the gospel lesson, which was about parents bringing their children to Jesus so that he might place his hands on them. As I read Mark 10:13, the melody of the old hymn "He Touched Me" played in my head. It's a hymn that always calls forth the memory of an experience with the elderly that gave me a new perspective on touch.

Soon after I assumed my role as a new pastor, the volunteer coordinator at the local health care facility asked if I would conduct worship services on a monthly rotation basis with other ministers. Since this was an important part of my church's outreach, I agreed, even though I had reservations about doing it. All of the elderly persons at the facility were strangers to me. None were even members of the church I was pastoring. I assumed many would be sight- and hearing-impaired. Some would be mentally confused. All would be weighed down by the heaviness of time as they waited out their days. What kind of sermon does one preach to a group like that? What message does one try to leave with them?

The day I arrived to conduct services for the first time, the coordinator explained what the service involved and that at the conclusion everyone joined in singing hymns. "Then it would be great if you could go around and greet each person," he said. "The residents love to have someone come in who reaches out and touches them."

I still remember being very uneasy with his suggestion. I had no feeling of connectedness with these people, no feeling of *us* or *we*; it was strictly a *them* and *me* situation.

The service began with a volunteer playing hymns on the piano. As I joined in the singing, I looked out at the residents who had gathered. Almost all of them were women. Several were secured in their wheelchairs with cloth ties. Many were toothless. An occasional one had a missing limb. *And I was supposed to go around and touch them!*

The hymn-singing was followed by prayers for individuals, after which a volunteer gave a devotional message. When it was my turn, I was introduced as the new pastor in town. Once I began preaching I relaxed and found the words that appeared to hold the interest of my audience. After I had finished, the coordinator announced the page number of the hymn. I was so focused on how I was going to weave among the wheelchairs and touch people that I didn't open the hymnal. The music began. I set forth feeling hesitant and unsure of myself. I reached for a gnarled hand here. Touched an arm or shoulder there, sometimes waking the person up.

At some point on my way around the room, I realized that the hymn being sung was "He Touched Me." Although it had long been one of my favorites, it suddenly took on new significance. At that moment I felt enfolded in God's grace and tears filled my eyes. In touching, I was being touched.

After the service I mentioned to the coordinator how affected I had been by the experience of greeting the residents to the accompaniment of "He Touched Me." From then on this hymn became my theme song and the coordinator always arranged to have it sung as I concluded the worship services to move among the residents, reaching out and touching each of them.

What Kind of Preacher
Is You, Anyway?

After an evening of church Bible study,
one of the parishioners came up to me and said, "Have I
got a story for you, Ron! This is one that'll preach." June
went on to say that each week she volunteers at a nursing
facility attached to a hospital and reads the Bible to the
residents. One elderly woman of whom she had grown
particularly fond was Maggie Jackson. "She tells me
stories and fills me in on what's happening in her life,"
June said. "She's nearly blind and loves having me read
the Bible to her. But last week when I went to see her, she
was really fussing."

It seems the hospital chaplain had stopped by to see
Maggie, and she asked him to sit down and read something
from his Bible. But the chaplain said, "I don't have a Bible
with me, Mrs. Jackson. Maybe I can read something from
yours."

"You don't have no *Bible*!" said a highly indignant
Maggie. "What kind of preacher is you, anyway?"

The fidgety chaplain offered to get one. "I'll be right
back," he promised.

"Don't you bother yourself," Maggie told him. "If
you're not the kind of preacher what brings his Bible, I
don't want to see you no more."

June and I laughed, and I agreed the story would indeed
preach. Little did I realize that much the same scenario
would play itself out in my own life that same day.

At noon a friend and I were having lunch in my office when I got an emergency call from the hospital. One of our parishioners was near death and I had to go immediately. I rushed to the reserved sacrament to get communion elements, got oils for anointing, picked up my Bible, and was on my way. At the hospital—after finally finding a parking space—I dashed to the intensive care waiting room where the family was gathered. We visited for a while, and then Stan's wife asked that I go in and pray with her husband. She said they have been reading the psalms together lately and thought that he would enjoy hearing me read them. "Right now Psalm 84 is a particular favorite," she said.

"Good, I'll read that one for sure." Then—like a brick falling on my head—I realized that I didn't have my Bible with me. Rushed as I had been, I had left it on the front seat of my car. So there I was on the eighth floor of the hospital ready to read a psalm to a dying man and I didn't have a Bible. In my head I heard Maggie Jackson saying, "What kind of preacher is you, anyway?"

Although I felt panicky, I tried to appear calm and excused myself for a moment. I went to the front desk and asked the nurse if she had a Bible. "I think there's one around here someplace," she said, and began searching under the counter. After what seemed a very long time, she triumphantly held up a copy of the Gideon Psalms and New Testament. That nurse would never know how grateful I was to be saved from joining the ranks of those not-to-be-taken-seriously preachers who show up without a Bible.

A *Truer Reflection*

❧

Everyone needs and likes to get positive
strokes, but I've found that if I start believing all the
affirmations it's like looking in a magnifying mirror in
which I'm larger than life. When this begins to happen,
someone is usually forthright enough to hold up a mirror
that gives a more realistic picture. I am reminded
especially of a time when I was doing a retreat on
spirituality in North Carolina. A young man named Bill
wrote to me beforehand saying he had read one of my early
books and hoped I would have time to visit with him
personally. I wrote back and told him that I was sure it
could be arranged.

During the week, Bill and I had several opportunities to
talk. On the final day of the retreat, he asked if we could
walk around the lake together. "I've got some things I'd
like to run past you," he said.

On the grounds outside the retreat center is a small lake
which, in my presentations, I had used as an analogy to
explain spiritual direction. I said that a spiritual director, or
companion on the way, is someone who has been around
the lake before and is therefore able to talk about the path,
to suggest places to pause, and to point out things to watch
for.

As Bill and I walked around the lake, he shared insights
he had gotten during the week and steps he thought he
might take. I commented freely, holding forth with
opinions and giving advice. At a certain point I must have
come across as just too all-knowing, because Bill placed a

silencing hand on my arm. "Hold on a minute, Ron," he said. "I didn't want to walk with the person who made the lake. I just wanted to walk with someone who had been around it a few times!"

I burst out laughing and so did Bill. He had hoped to benefit from my experience, but I was the one who benefited most because he was honest enough to take away the magnifying mirror and hold up one that gave a truer reflection.

Channels for God's Love

I first met Barbara when she was about
twelve years old and a member of the parish where I was
the pastor. An attractive, vibrant girl with honey-colored
hair, she had a keen interest in theater and acting. After
graduating from high school, she went off to college and I
moved. For about two years we had no contact with one
another. Then to my surprise and delight, she called one
day saying she wanted to talk. Although Barbara was a
deeply spiritual young woman with a rich prayer life, she
said she wasn't attending church. As she put it, "There just
doesn't seem to be any place where I fit in."

During the course of that year, Barbara called me four or
five times and we talked about what was going on in her
life. Occasionally she wrote a note. But then the calls and
notes stopped. I did not know how to reach her by phone.
And when I tried writing, my letter was returned stamped
"No forwarding address."

Again, almost two years passed before I heard from
Barbara. This time her call was from Detroit, where she had
been living for over a year. We started the conversation by
catching up on what had happened since we last talked.
Barbara's life was in transition: she was moving to a new
apartment and beginning a new job and had recently broken
up with the boyfriend she had been seeing for several
months. Although she was making an effort to be
lighthearted, the tone of her voice told me that something
was wrong. While continuing to hold up my end of the
conversation, I asked God to help Barbara reveal what was

weighing on her heart and let her know that I would do whatever I could to help.

After a little more small talk, Barbara blurted, "Ron, I had an abortion." Neither of us spoke for several seconds. Then in a voice strained with emotion, Barbara said that when she told her boyfriend about the pregnancy he rejected her, and she was left to face the situation alone. She talked to friends who gave her various pieces of advice, and finally she decided on the abortion. "It happened several months ago," she said, "but now I don't feel at all good about what I did." Although she had confessed before God, the deep sadness in her soul remained.

"Barbara," I said, "it sounds like you want to go to confession."

She gave a little gasp. "Yes! Yes!," she said excitedly. "That's what I want. But can we do it?"

A confession over the phone wasn't what I had in mind. Barbara had already confessed to God and to me. What she needed now was to meet with someone who would reach out and touch her as Jesus so often did in his healing ministry. She needed to be told, "Barbara, God has forgiven you, and in the name of Jesus Christ, I forgive you."

It was one thing to know what Barbara needed and quite another to make it happen. After all, she was in Detroit and I was in Birmingham. Then I remembered that a friend of mine had just moved to Birmingham from Detroit. Possibly Bill knew someone who could be of help. I explained what I had in mind, and Barbara liked the idea. I told her I would call her in an hour. I feel strongly that the events that followed were not just luck or happenstance but evidence of God's grace and powerful spirit at work.

I was able to reach my friend Bill and explained the

situation to him. "Where does she live?" he asked. When I told him, he said, "Just the next parish from her neighborhood is a priest I think would be helpful."

Bill gave me her name and I promptly called the church where she was on the staff. The secretary said it was her day off, but gave me her home number and suggested I call her there. I reached her on my first try and she was delighted that I had contacted her. During the past two years, the focus of her ministry had been on women who had been abused or raped or were suffering the emotional aftereffects of abortion. She even had a support group for young women who had been involved in sexual incidents and needed nurturing and reassurance.

I called Barbara back and gave her the priest's name and number. "She will be waiting for your call," I said. "I think you two will really connect, and she'll be able to give you what you need just now."

The more we reach out to others, the more we recognize the need for referrals and the necessity of asking for suggestions and help. By involving others in our efforts, we experience a connectedness with a variety of caring people and a growing awareness that we are not alone in serving the hungry, the hurting, the fearful, the lonely, and the many others in need. A large number of people become our allies and the channels through which God's love can flow.

Appendix

Times of Change,
Times of Challenge

After a church supper, a parishioner in

his late forties approached me. Instead of his usual glad-to-see-you smile, there was a tense set to Howard's mouth and a weary look in his eyes. "How are things going?" I asked, hoping the question was an invitation to talk about what was bothering him.

"We're having a rough time at our house," Howard said. "Lora's mother is staying with us. She hasn't been well, and we're concerned about her living alone way off in Arizona. For quite a while we've been trying to convince her to move in with us, but now that she's been here for a couple of weeks we know it just won't work."

At that point in our conversation, one of Howard's children wanted his attention. I suggested he give me a call and we would set a time to talk; he could come to my office or we could meet for lunch. I said that if he thought it would be helpful to involve the whole family, I would be glad to drop by their home. Howard thanked me for my offer, but I sensed he wouldn't follow through. He and his family were very private people, and without some initiative on Howard's part, I knew that I probably shouldn't pursue the matter either—at least not at that time.

As pastors, we quickly discover that a great many of our parishioners who have a particular concern come to us only once. Frequently, they tell us their problem in a hurried exchange after church or at a social function such as the one Howard chose. They might intend to follow up and so might we. But more often than not they don't. Perhaps they feel they would be imposing on us, and we don't want to impose on them.

I have often thought how helpful it would be if we had booklets dealing with specific concerns to give to parishioners. One day over lunch I mentioned this to a group of laypeople from the parish who immediately asked, "Why just for pastors? They aren't the only ones who would find them helpful." Then they asked what topics I was thinking of. Their enthusiasm for the titles I had in mind let me know that what I had perceived as a need for pastors was a need for others as well, especially for relatives, neighbors, close friends, lay visitors for the church, and other caregivers who are often overlooked.

Initially I had envisioned these booklets on bookshelves in the pastor's office. Now I also saw them on racks in bookstores and churches and on loan in church libraries. I wanted to create something that would be both practical and uplifting. Out of this desire was born the *Times of Change, Times of Challenge* series that is being introduced with the following titles:

When an Aging Loved One Needs Care
When You Are Facing Surgery
When You Are Getting Married
When Your Child Is Baptized

Had these booklets been available when Howard spoke with me, I could have followed up our conversation by sending him *When an Aging Loved One Needs Care*. I would have included a personal note with the booklet.

Harriet made an appointment to see me because she was troubled about the surgery she faced. How I wish that before she left my office I could have reached back to my shelf and handed her *When You Are Facing Surgery*. The thoughts in this booklet would have been an extension of our conversation and given her encouragement and comfort as she prepared for surgery. The booklet would also have helped during her convalescence.

Although marriage and the baptism of a child are times of joy, they also are times of change and challenge. When we give a booklet to an engaged couple or to parents whose baby is to be baptized, we are helping them mark important milestones in their lives while at the same time giving them information that will aid them in meeting their new challenges.

During both the joyful and the difficult times of their lives, our people want to feel that they are not alone. They want to know that their pastor, along with the rest of their faith community, is walking with them. I believe that all of us—pastors and parishioners alike—are born to let the love of God shine through us into the lives of others. The kindness and caring we show one another, the shared laughter and the shared tears are God's way of fulfilling the promise "I am with you always" (Matt. 28:20, RSV).

Resource Networking

The woman on the phone introduced

herself as Peggy Samuels and said she was looking for a
co-dependency group, but not one that dealt with a specific
addiction. And she didn't want one that was led by a
therapist.

My mind went blank. I had no resources whatever to
suggest. I asked for her number and said I would return her
call.

After hanging up, I called a therapist from my parish
who works in co-dependency and addictions. I told her
what I was looking for and she directed me to a new group,
giving me time, place, and phone number. I promptly called
Peggy with the information. In amazement, she said, "My
friend Sylvia was right when she told me that if anybody
would know, you would."

As I hung up the phone, I thought about how my
perception of my ministry has changed over time. In the
early years, I believed that I had to be all things to all
people; I was supposed to have the answer to everyone's
problem. In retrospect, I can see that part of this feeling
came about because back then there were far fewer church
and community support services. Basically there were
groups for alcoholics, for troubled adolescents, and for
couples wanting to strengthen their marriages.

The past decade has seen a mushrooming of support
groups and organizations that deal with everything from
specific illnesses to single parenthood, from physical
handicaps to a variety of compulsive behaviors. We have

also seen an increase in the number and variety of church support groups as well as government and community social service programs. With all these groups and services available, I have come to see that I can most effectively meet the needs of my parishioners through resource networking. If I can't give the necessary information or ongoing support, I am usually able to make a referral where they can find the help they need.

When I moved into a small community, the pastor from a neighboring parish gave me a copy of the county's resource guide which contained names, addresses, and phone numbers for various agencies and services. I found this guide to be invaluable. When I am looking for social services in the city, I use the yellow pages and the listing for county, state, and federal government offices and agencies. In many cities, the United Way or a similar agency has a First Call for Help number. The representative answering the phone directs the caller to the proper agency, service, or group to meet a specific need. But as I did with Peggy, the first call I make is usually to a friend, colleague, or parishioner. Invariably they give whatever help they can, knowing that when they request my help, I will respond in kind.

The appendix of this book lists a number of help-giving organizations. This listing is not meant to be all-inclusive, but it does indicate just how numerous and varied are the organizations whose aim is to help people help themselves. I request printed material from the organizations my parishioners seek out most frequently and keep the leaflets on hand. I find it is much more supportive to provide information immediately than to just give an address or phone number.

Help-Giving Organizations

A wide variety of organizations offer their help to anyone who needs it. The organizations I have selected to include in this list are merely a cross section of what is available. For additional help see the *Encyclopedia of Associations*, which can be found in the reference section of most public libraries. This three-volume set contains a comprehensive listing of all the national organizations found in the United States.

Most of the organizations listed below are nonprofit. When requesting information, enclose a self-addressed, stamped envelope.

- **Abuse**

PARENTS AGAINST MOLESTERS
PO BOX 3557
PORTSMOUTH VA 23701
(For molestation victims, their families, and concerned individuals)

PARENTS ANONYMOUS
6733 SEPULVEDAS STE 270
LOS ANGELES CA 90045
(For abusive parents)

SURVIVORS OF INCEST ANONYMOUS
PO BOX 21817
BALTIMORE MD 21222
(For incest survivors, a 12-step recovery group)

VOICES IN ACTION
PO BOX 148309
CHICAGO IL 60614
(For adult survivors of incest and sexual abuse as children, and
for spouses, relatives, and concerned citizens)

- **Adoption**

COMMITTEE FOR SINGLE ADOPTIVE PARENTS
PO BOX 15084
CHEVY CHASE MD 20815
(For single persons who have adopted or wish to adopt children)

YESTERDAY'S CHILDREN
PO BOX 1554
EVANSTON IL 60204
(For persons seeking to be reunited with their biological
families)

- **Aging**

CHILDREN OF AGING PARENTS
2761 TRENTON RD
LEVITTOWN PA 19059
(Self-help group concerned with the education, support,
guidance, and development of coping skills of caregivers of the
elderly)

- **AIDS**

AIDS CLINICAL TRIALS GROUP
NATIONAL INSTITUTE OF HEALTH
6003 EXECUTIVE BLVD RM 200P
ROCKVILLE MD 20852
(For persons interested in enrolling in experimental AIDS
treatment programs)

NATIONAL AIDS INFORMATION CLEARINGHOUSE
PO BOX 6003
ROCKVILLE MD 20850
(For AIDS/HIV information, resources, and publications)

NATIONAL ASSOCIATION OF PEOPLE WITH AIDS
2025 I ST NW STE 1118
WASHINGTON DC 20006
(Self-improvement programs for persons with AIDS, AIDS-Related Complex, or HIV)

PROJECT INFORM
347 DOLORES STE 301
SAN FRANCISCO CA 94110
(Latest information on HIV/AIDS treatment)

- **Arthritis**

ARTHRITIS FOUNDATION
1314 SPRING ST NW
ATLANTA GA 30309
(For arthritics of all ages and their families)

- **Asthma**

NATIONAL FOUNDATION FOR ASTHMA
PO BOX 30069
TUCSON AZ 85751
(For asthmatics of all ages)

MOTHERS OF ASTHMATICS
10875 MAIN ST RM 210
FAIRFAX VA 22030
(For parents of asthmatic children)

- **Autism**

AUTISM SOCIETY OF AMERICA
1234 MASSACHUSETTS AVE NW STE C-1017
WASHINGTON DC 20005
(For parents with autistic children and others interested in the disorder)

- **Cancer**

AMERICAN CANCER SOCIETY
1599 CLIFTON RD NE
ATLANTA GA 30329
(For cancer patients and anyone interested in cancer education)

CANDLELIGHTERS CHILDHOOD CANCER FOUNDATION
1312 18 ST NW
WASHINGTON DC 20036
(For parents whose children have or have had cancer)

MAKE TODAY COUNT
101½ UNION ST S
ALEXANDRIA VA 22314
(For cancer patients and their immediate families)

REACH TO RECOVERY
C/o AMERICAN CANCER SOCIETY
1599 CLIFTON RD NE
ATLANTA GA 30329
(For women who have had breast cancer)

- **Chemical Dependency**

AL-ANON FAMILY GROUP HEADQUARTERS
PO BOX 862 MIDTOWN STATION
NEW YORK NY 10018
(For families of alcoholics)

ALATEEN
PO BOX 862 MIDTOWN STATION
NEW YORK NY 10018
(For teenage children of alcoholics)

ALCOHOLICS ANONYMOUS
AA WORLD SERVICES
PO BOX 459 GRAND CENTRAL STATION
NEW YORK NY 10163
(For adult alcoholics)

NATIONAL ASSOCIATION FOR CHILDREN OF
   ALCOHOLICS
31582 COAST HWY STE B
SOUTH LAGUNA CA 92677
(For individuals of all ages who are children of alcoholics)

DRUGS ANONYMOUS
PO BOX 473 ANSONIA STATION
NEW YORK NY 10023
(For persons addicted to drugs including tranquilizers and
stimulants)

FAMILIES IN ACTION
NATIONAL DRUG INFORMATION CENTER
2296 HENDERSON MILL RD STE 204
ATLANTA GA 30345
(For parents and other adults concerned with preventing drug
abuse)

NARCOTICS ANONYMOUS
PO BOX 9999
VAN NUYS CA 91409
(For recovering drug addicts)

- **Chronic Fatigue**

INTERNATIONAL CHRONIC FATIGUE SYNDROME
  SOCIETY
PO BOX 230108
PORTLAND OR 97223
(For persons with CFS—formerly referred to as Epstein-Barr
Virus Syndrome—their families and others interested in the
disease)

- **Chronic Pain**

NATIONAL CHRONIC PAIN OUTREACH ASSOCIATION
4922 HAMPDEN LANE
BETHESDA MD 20814
(Emotional support for persons who suffer chronic pain and for
their families)

- **Cystic Fibrosis**

CYSTIC FIBROSIS FOUNDATION
6931 ARLINGTON RD RM 200
BETHESDA MD 20814

- **Death & Grief**

THE COMPASSIONATE FRIENDS
PO BOX 3696
OAK BROOK IL 60522-3696
(For parents who have experienced the death of a child.
Non-denominational)

PREGNANCY AND INFANT LOSS CENTER
1421 WAYZATA BLVD E RM 40
WAYZATA MN 55391
(For parents who have suffered a miscarriage, stillbirth, or infant
death)

NATIONAL SUDDEN INFANT DEATH SYNDROME
  FOUNDATION
10500 PATUXENT PKWY RM 420
COLUMBIA MD 21044
(For parents and families of children who die from SIDS,
sometimes referred to as "crib death")

INTERNATIONAL ASSOCIATION FOR WIDOWED PEOPLE
PO BOX 3564
SPRINGFIELD IL 62708
(For widowed persons and their families who are coping with grief)

• Debt

DEBTORS ANONYMOUS
PO BOX 20322
NEW YORK NY 10025
(For men and women who share the common problem of
compulsive debting)

• Diabetes

AMERICAN DIABETES ASSOCIATION
1660 DUKE ST PO BOX 25757
ALEXANDRIA VA 22314
(For diabetics of all ages and their families)

JUVENILE DIABETES FOUNDATION INTERNATIONAL
432 PARK AVE S
NEW YORK NY 10016
(For juvenile diabetics and their families)

• Eating Disorders

ANOREXIA NERVOSA AND RELATED EATING DISORDERS
PO BOX 5102
EUGENE OR 97405
(For anorectics, bulimics, their families and friends)

OVEREATERS ANONYMOUS
PO BOX 92870
LOS ANGELES CA 90009
(For men and women who are compulsive eaters)

- **Epilepsy**

EPILEPSY FOUNDATION OF AMERICA
4351 GARDEN CITY DR
LANDOVER MD 20785
(For epileptics of all ages and their families)

- **Gambling**

GAM-ANON FOR INTERNATIONAL SERVICE OFFICE
PO BOX 157
WHITESTONE NY 11357
(For families of compulsive gamblers)

GAMBLERS ANONYMOUS
3255 WILSHIRE BLVD RM 610
LOS ANGELES CA 90010
(For men and women seeking help with their compulsive gambling.)

- **Hearing Disabilities**

ALEXANDER GRAHAM BELL ASSOCIATION FOR THE
  DEAF
3417 VOLTA PLACE NW
WASHINGTON DC 20007
(For hearing-impaired adults and parents of deaf children)

AMERICAN EAR ASSOCIATION FOR RESEARCH
C/o DR PAUL YANICK JR
RR3 BOX 290F
LAKE ARIEL PA 18436
(For adults and children who suffer from tinnitus and hearing-related problems)

- **Heart Conditions**

AMERICAN HEART ASSOCIATION
7320 GREENVILLE AVE
DALLAS TX 75231
(For persons with heart ailments and their families)

MENDED HEARTS
c/o AMERICAN HEART ASSOCIATION
7320 GREENVILLE AVE
DALLAS TX 75231
(For persons who have heart disease, their families and friends)

- **Huntington's Disease**

HUNTINGTON'S DISEASE SOCIETY OF AMERICA
140 W 22 ST 6TH FLOOR
NEW YORK NY 10011-2420
(For persons with Huntington's disease and their families)

- **Ileitis & Colitis**

NATIONAL FOUNDATION FOR ILEITIS AND COLITIS
444 PARK AVE S 11TH FLOOR
NEW YORK NY 10016
(For persons with ileitis and colitis and their families)

- **Incarceration**

PRISON FAMILIES ANONYMOUS
353 FULTON AVE
HEMPSTEAD NY 11550
(For families and close friends of those involved in the criminal or juvenile justice system)

- **Kidney**

AMERICAN ASSOCIATION OF KIDNEY PATIENTS
1 DAVIS BLVD STE LL1
TAMPA FL 33606
(For persons with kidney disorders, their families and friends)

• Learning Disabilities

NATIONAL INSTITUTE OF DYSLEXIA
PO BOX 10487
ROCKVILLE MD 20850
(For parents of dyslexic children and adults wanting information
about the disorder)

ASSOCIATION FOR CHILDREN AND ADULTS WITH
  LEARNING DISABILITIES
4156 LIBRARY RD
PITTSBURGH PA 15236

• Lung

AMERICAN LUNG ASSOCIATION
1740 BROADWAY
NEW YORK NY 10019
(For persons with lung disorders)

• Lupus

LUPUS FOUNDATION OF AMERICA
1717 MASSACHUSETTS AVE NW STE 203
WASHINGTON DC 20036
(For persons with lupus erythematosus and their families)

• Mental Conditions

ALZHEIMER'S ASSOCIATION
702 E LAKE ST STE 600
CHICAGO IL 60601
(For families who have a member with Alzheimer's disease)

ASSOCIATION FOR RETARDED CITIZENS
PO BOX 6109
ARLINGTON TX 76005
(For parents, professional workers, and others interested in
individuals with mental retardation)

NATIONAL ALLIANCE FOR THE MENTALLY ILL
2101 WILSON BLVD STE 302
ARLINGTON VA 22201
(Refers the mentally ill to local programs)

NATIONAL DEPRESSIVE AND MANIC DEPRESSIVE
    ASSOCIATION
53 JACKSON BLVD W RM 618
CHICAGO IL 60604
(For manic depressive patients and their families)

AMERICAN SCHIZOPHRENIA ASSOCIATION
900 FEDERAL HWY N STE 330
BOCA RATON FL 33432
(For schizophrenics and their families)

- **Missing Children**

FIND THE CHILDREN
11811 OLYMPIC BLVD W
LOS ANGELES CA 90064
(For families of missing children)

- **Multiple Births**

NATIONAL ORGANIZATION OF MOTHERS OF TWINS
    CLUBS
12404 PRINCESS JEANNE NE
ALBUQUERQUE NM 87112
(For parents of twins)

TRIPLET CONNECTION
PO BOX 99571
STOCKTON CA 95209
(For parents and expectant parents of triplets or large multiple
births)

- ## Multiple Sclerosis

NATIONAL MULTIPLE SCLEROSIS SOCIETY
205 E 42 ST
NEW YORK NY 10017
(For persons with multiple sclerosis and their families)

- ## Outreach

HABITAT FOR HUMANITY INTERNATIONAL
HABITAT AND CHURCH STS
AMERICUS GA 31709
(Ecumenical Christian organization dedicated to providing low-cost, non-profit housing to low-income people throughout the world)

NATIONAL RARE BLOOD CLUB
c/o ASSOCIATED HEALTH FOUNDATION
164 5 AVE
NEW YORK NY 10010
(For persons ages 18–65 with rare blood types who are physically able to donate blood)

PEACE CORPS
1990 K ST NW
WASHINGTON DC 20526
(Independent federal agency seeking volunteers to promote peace and friendship in various parts of the world)

- ## Prison Ministries

KAIROS INC
1298 MINNESOTA AVE
WINTER PARK FL 32789
(Ecumenical three-day in-prison retreat program with monthly followup)

PRISON FELLOWSHIP MINISTRIES
PO BOX 17500
WASHINGTON DC 20041
(Encourages Christians to work in prisons and to assist communities in ministering to prisoners, ex-offenders, and their families)

RE-ENTRY MINISTRIES INC
PO BOX 100461
BIRMINGHAM AL 35210
(Primarily assisting ex-offenders as they return to the community from prison and assisting their families)

- **Paget's Disease**

PAGET'S DISEASE FOUNDATION
PO BOX 2772
BROOKLYN NY 11202
(For persons with Paget's disease and their families)

- **Parkinson's Disease**

AMERICAN PARKINSON DISEASE ASSOCIATION
116 JOHN ST STE 417
NEW YORK NY 10038
(For persons with Parkinson's disease and their families)

- **Physical Disability/Disfigurement**

NATIONAL SPINAL CORD INJURY ASSOCIATION
600 CUMMINGS PARK W STE 2000
WOBURN MA 01801
(For persons with spinal cord injuries and their families)

NATIONAL WHEELCHAIR ATHLETIC ASSOCIATION
1604 PIKES PEAK AVE E
COLORADO SPRINGS CO 80909
(For men and women who compete in various amateur sports in wheelchairs)

NATIONAL FOUNDATION FOR FACIAL
  RECONSTRUCTION
317 34 ST E STE 901
NEW YORK NY 10016
(For persons who have been facially disfigured)

• Rare Disorders

NATIONAL ORGANIZATION FOR RARE DISORDERS
PO BOX 8923
NEW FAIRFIELD CT 06812
(For persons seeking information about rare disorders)

• Reye's Syndrome

NATIONAL REYE'S SYNDROME FOUNDATION
426 N LEWIS PO BOX 829
BRYAN OH 43506
(For families of children with Reye's Syndrome)

• Scleroderma

SCLERODERMA FEDERATION
1725 YORK AVE RM 29F
NEW YORK NY 10128
(For scleroderma patients and their families

• Scoliosis

SCOLIOSIS ASSOCIATION
PO BOX 51353
RALEIGH NC 27609
(For persons with, or interested in, scoliosis)

• Senior Citizens

ASSOCIATION OF INFORMED SENIOR CITIZENS
560 HERNDON PKWY STE 110
HERNDON VA 22070
(Consumer interest group for persons 55 and older)

AMERICAN ASSOCIATION OF RETIRED PERSONS
1909 K ST NW
WASHINGTON DC 20049
(Offers a wide range of services to persons over age 50)

• Sex

SEXAHOLICS ANONYMOUS
PO BOX 300
SIMI VALLEY CA 93062
(For individuals wishing to stop their sexually self-destructive
behavior)

COALITION ON SEXUALITY AND DISABILITY
132 23 ST E
NEW YORK NY 10010
(Promotes sexual health care services for persons with disabilities)

• Sickle Cell Disease

NATIONAL ASSOCIATION FOR SICKLE CELL DISEASE
4221 WILSHIRE BLVD STE 360
LOS ANGELES CA 90010
(For community groups involved in sickle cell anemia programs
throughout the U.S.)

• Sight Disabilities

MYOPIA INTERNATIONAL RESEARCH FOUNDATION
1265 BROADWAY RM 608
NEW YORK NY 10001
(For nearsighted persons and their families)

ASSOCIATED SERVICES FOR THE BLIND
919 WALNUT ST
PHILADELPHIA PA 19107
(Provides services that foster independent living for the blind
and visually impaired)

NATIONAL ASSOCIATION FOR PARENTS OF THE
   VISUALLY IMPAIRED
2180 LINWAY
BELOIT WI 53511

- **Singles**

NATIONAL ASSOCIATION OF CHRISTIAN SINGLES
1933 WISCONSIN AVE W
MILWAUKEE WI 53233
(For unmarried, divorced, and widowed adults)

PARENTS WITHOUT PARTNERS
8807 COLESVILLE RD
SILVER SPRINGS MD 20910
(For single parents)

- **Sjogren's Syndrome**

SJOGREN'S SYNDROME FOUNDATION
382 MAIN ST
PORT WASHINGTON
NEW YORK NY 11050

- **Sleep Disorders**

AMERICAN SLEEP DISORDERS ASSOCIATION
604 2 ST SW
ROCHESTER MN 55902
(Diagnostic and treatment services for persons with sleep disorders)

- **Smoking**

CITIZENS AGAINST TOBACCO SMOKE
PO BOX 36236
CINCINNATI OH 45236
(For persons concerned with indoor pollution caused by tobacco
smoke)

- **Spina Bifida**

SPINA BIFIDA ASSOCIATION OF AMERICA
1700 ROCKVILLE PIKE STE 540
ROCKVILLE MD 20852
(For persons with spina bifida, their parents, relatives, and friends)

- **Stroke**

STROKE CLUBS INTERNATIONAL
805 12 ST
GALVESTON TX 77550
(For persons who have had strokes and their families)

- **Stuttering**

NATIONAL STUTTERING PROJECT
4601 IRVING ST
SAN FRANCISCO CA 94122-1020
(Self-help organization for people who stutter, parents of children who stutter, and speech pathologists)